The
HAPPY
Toddler Book

A Dorling Kindersley Book

100 ways to keep your toddler smiling

Introduction – Tommy's Campaign

quiet times

*Ideas 1-2, 34, 82,
95-98 and 100*

including: • relaxed mornings
and evenings • enjoying books
and photos

energy busters

*Ideas 20, 29-30, 32-33,
80, 86-88, 92 and 94*

including: • party fun • rough
and tumble • action rhymes
• ball games and pillow fights

pretend play

*Ideas 31, 48-59,
72 and 99*

including: • dressing up, dancing
and movement • helping with
chores in the house and garden
• looking after a play pet
• putting teddy to bed

out and about

*Ideas 35-47, 73-74
and 89-91*

including: • pottering in the
garden • growing a sunflower
• going for a nature walk
• visiting the zoo • fun in the
rain • choosing a pet

things to make

*Ideas 6, 8-10, 11-14,
21-25, 75-79 and 83-84*

including: • baking playdough
and making models from
junk • creating amazing
masks, hats and crazy faces
• puppets, printing
and painting

food fun

toys and games

Dorling Kindersley

LONDON, NEW YORK, SYDNEY, DELHI,
PARIS, MUNICH and JOHANNESBURG

Senior Managing Art Editor Lynne Brown

Senior Managing Editor Corinne Roberts

Art Editor Glenda Fisher

Project Editor Valerie Kitchenham

DTP Designer Rajen Shah

Production Joanna Bull

First published in Great Britain in 2000
by Dorling Kindersley Limited,
9 Henrietta Street, Covent Garden,
London WC2E 8PS

Copyright © 2000 Dorling Kindersley Limited,
London

ISBN 0 7513 0895 1

Reproduced by Colourscan, Singapore.
Printed and bound by
South China Printing Co. Ltd

see our complete catalogue at
www.dk.com

Introduction

Every day, thousands of people experience the thrill of becoming parents to a healthy baby who will bring them no end of joy. And for those parents, a primary concern will be to ensure that their baby remains healthy, happy and stimulated, nurtured by an environment that offers limitless opportunities for development through learning and play. This is where *The Happy Toddler Book* can help. Packed with 100 ideas for keeping a toddler amused, it is designed to inspire parents, grandparents, aunties, uncles and carers alike.

Sadly, however, not everyone is fortunate enough to experience the joy of having a happy, healthy baby and the sorrow and heartache felt at the loss of a tiny life is indescribable. This is where **Tommy's Campaign** – a national charity, funding medical research into the causes of stillbirth, premature birth and miscarriage – has a vital role to contribute. The charity also provides helpful information and literature for parents and for those who are thinking about starting a family.

The single aim of **Tommy's Campaign** is to give babies a better start in life by making pregnancy and birth healthier and safer for baby and mother. It's astounding to learn that every year in the UK alone:

- 1 in 5 pregnancies ends in miscarriage
- 1 in 188 babies is tragically lost through stillbirth
- 100 babies a day are born too small or too soon.

It is also sobering to realise that these figures haven't really changed since the 1930's, so the need for medical research remains as urgent as ever. **Tommy's Campaign** receives no government funding, which means that without your generosity the charity would not be able to support the research projects that are needed throughout the UK. For every copy sold of *The Happy Toddler Book*, 13p will go to **Tommy's Campaign**.

Thank you for your support in helping to give every baby the best possible start in life.

Finding the answers to problem pregnancies

Registered charity number 1060508

For information on **Tommy's Campaign**, you can call 020 7620 0188 or write to: Tommy's Campaign, Freepost (Lon 1053), London SE99 6RD. Using a stamp will save the charity money. For details on how to join 'smalltalk', Tommy's Campaign's new club for parents, just turn to the back of this book.

The fun

starts here...

1

rise and shine

Your toddler's mood first thing in the morning can determine how the rest of her day develops. Whenever you can it's a good idea to make the effort to get things off to a leisurely – and therefore less stressful – start. It might sound impossible, particularly if you both have to be out of the door by 8am, but if you can get up twenty minutes earlier you will find it pays dividends. Use the time to snuggle up together in your dressing gowns and have a chat or play with teddies. A gentle start gives you special time together and leaves you both in a positive mood to face the day.

2
let him do it himself

Your toddler wants to do it and to do
it now, *by himself*. So, on days when
you don't have to rush out
anywhere, let him dress himself.
It doesn't matter if his top is on
back to front or he's wearing odd
socks – you can perfect his
high-fashion look later! Instead,
share in his triumph at having
negotiated tricky arm holes.

3

give him a pull toy...

A pull-along toy goes where you go – it stops when you stop, like a very obedient pet. Your toddler will revel in his power over cause and effect. He pulls, the toy follows, and it makes a satisfying noise. Above all, the toy is your child's companion as he toddles about his business.

4

...and his own set of wheels

As soon as he can sit safely astride one, a ride-on toy is a must for a toddler with places to go. Whether you borrow one from the toy library or buy him his own, it will always be a favourite. Small wooden trikes are a good start, so that your toddler can propel himself along with his feet. When he is older he will be able to master a real trike with pedals. Good exercise for him — and for you as you race to catch up!

5

let him have a bash...

...with a hammering toy. It will use up some of that excess energy and it's a great way to improve your toddler's manual dexterity and hand-eye co-ordination, even if it is a bit tough on your nerves! This activity is shape-sorting with a difference – while your toddler learns to match the holes with the shapes, he has the satisfaction of bashing out lots of noise.

6

bake playdough

You will need: 1 teacup of plain flour; 2 tsp cream of tartar;
½ teacup of salt; 1 tbsp vegetable oil; 1 teacup of water; a few
drops of food colouring. Mix together the dry ingredients, then
add the oil. Mix well, then add the water. When you have a
smooth paste, add the colouring. Heat the mixture in a pan until
it is doughy and comes away from the sides. Let it cool and then
knead before using. Store, covered, in the fridge.

play

smiling

sad

surprised

copycat faces

laughing

excited

cheeky

Make an amazing mask from...

8

a paper bag

Start by holding a paper bag up against your toddler's head. Mark where her eyes are in relation to the bag, then take the bag away *before* cutting out small eye holes. Help your toddler to paint the bag with a funny face, sticking on hair and ears if you want to.

a paper plate

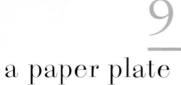

Take a paper plate, cut out eye holes, and help
your toddler to decorate it with a face. If you prefer, cut out
a half mask (as shown above). Attach an elastic
headband, so the mask is easy to wear.

bright tissue paper

With a paper plate as the base, your toddler can have great fun
creating a tissue-paper mask. Cut out a nose or beak from card
and glue it on. Make eye holes and add an elastic headband.

paint a crazy face

Just like dressing up, having her face painted lets your toddler adopt a disguise and means she can explore different feelings as she pretends to be a cat, a clown or a superhero. You will need to decorate her face for her using special face-painting make-up sticks that are available from most toy shops and toy superstores. Don't feel the need to attempt too ambitious a design – your toddler will be just as thrilled with something simple. For extra fun, buy some face glitter and experiment with adding some sparkle to your range of funny faces.

12

make him king for a day...

Perfect for a party or for the dressing-up box, a regal crown is easy to make. Take a band of card – if it has a metallic finish, so much the better – about 15cm (6in) wide that fits around your child's head. Cut deep 'V' shapes into it to create points. Paint gold, if needed, and finish with jewel shapes cut from foil.

13

...or a wonderful wizard

Measure around your child's head with string. Lay string in a curve on black card; trace curve with a pencil. Measuring up from either end of this curve, draw two lines to meet in a point. Cut out the fan shape you've made. Fold to create a cone; secure with sticky tape. Decorate with moons and stars.

go clowning around!

A giant pair of clown's trousers will make a comical addition to your toddler's dressing-up box. Go to a jumble sale or charity shop and find a pair of trousers, the brighter the better, with a very large waist. Then sew a hoop into the waistband and roll up the bottoms. A wide pair of braces will add an authentic final touch.

You don't to

party to play...

15

pin the tail on the donkey

All you need is a blackboard or a large sheet of paper with a donkey, or any other favourite animal, drawn on it. Cut out a tail and put a blob of adhesive putty on the back. Blindfold your toddler with a scarf, then ask her to stick on the tail.

16

paperchain congas

Take a piece of paper and fold it concertina-style, until you've
used up the whole sheet and have a rectangle of layers. Using
scissors, cut leg shapes out of the bottom edge of the rectangle,
arm shapes out of the sides, and a head out of the top. Unfold
to show your toddler the conga of paper people!

17

follow the leader

This is a case of the more the merrier, but you can play with
as few as two toddlers if you like. Pop on some fun music
and watch the followers copy whatever the leader does…

18

what's in
the parcel?

Wrap up half a dozen or so familiar household objects using
paper and string, then ask your toddler and her friends to
guess what each one is. For the sake of variety, make some
objects easy to work out and others more of a challenge.

19

pass the parcel!

With this game, it's the fun of unwrapping that is appealing.
Wrap the prize in layers of paper, pass around to music, then
whoever has the parcel when the music stops gets to unwrap
a layer. Keep going until finally
the gift is revealed.

20
make her star

Conjure up a magical star and moon theme party for your toddler and her friends. Make decorations (like those shown here) from gold and silver paper. Take a length of card that fits around your child's head and glue to make a headband –

of the show

attach a star or moon to the front and repeat to make party
hats for all the guests. Make magic wands from lengths of
dowelling with card stars glued on the end. And serve
sandwiches and biscuits cut using a star-shaped pastry cutter.

Use household junk to make...

...a pair of binoculars

Collect cardboard packets and tubes, egg boxes and plastic bottles and, with your help, your toddler can create junk models. Make binoculars by gluing two toilet-roll tubes to either side of disks of glued-together thick card. Then create hand-grips from corrugated paper and a neck-strap from a length of string.

22 ...giant shakers

Using poster paint mixed with PVA glue, decorate two large empty plastic bottles with crazy patterns. Let the paint dry, pour in some dry rice, secure the bottle tops, and get shaking!

23 ...a space rocket

Paint a cardboard tube a solid colour, then add a door and some windows. Cut out a circle of card, cut into the central point, and fold into a cone; glue. Stick the cone on top of the rocket body. Glue red and orange tissue paper engine flames around the rocket base. You have lift off!

24 ...a sports car

Let your toddler live life in the fast lane! Get hold of a suitably large cardboard box and then have fun together customizing it. Use paper plates for wheels, foil pie dishes for mirrors and headlights, and attach a toy or home-made steering wheel. Pop a small chair inside and she'll be off...

25 ...a secret den

Choose a very large box and cut out windows for your toddler to peep through – you could even glue up squares of material to make window and door curtains. For extra special fun, serve up the following delicious snacks for in-den dining...

26

funny face snack

Den food should be fun to eat. Top a pizza base or omelette with sieved tomato and cheese, and decorate with a silly face.

27

chunky cheese straws

Roll out some puff pastry; brush with egg. Sprinkle cheese over half the pastry, fold to make a 'sandwich', roll flat; brush with egg. Cut into strips; twist each several times. Bake on a greased tray for 10 minutes at 220°C/425°F/Gas Mark 7.

28

fruity jelly pots

Make up some jelly. Pop fresh fruit pieces into the bottom of individual plastic bowls, then top with jelly. Leave to set.

29

get into the groove!

Every toddler loves dancing, and having a boogie around the room will brighten up any low moment. For a real giggle, try dancing with your toddler's feet resting on top of your own. See how long you can keep in step, changing direction and going backwards and sideways, too.

... do a roly-poly

30

There's no alternative — you'll have to get down on the floor to show her how to do this one! Don't worry if she can't do a full roly-poly, it's fun just to have a go. Whatever you do, never be tempted to force her over. Every child's co-ordination develops at a different rate, so give her time.

put her in the spotlight

For the serious dancer, there's nothing like the romance of the ballet. Whether it's the chance to be the centre of attention or just the appeal of wearing a tutu, your toddler will love to dress up and dance. And it's not just the girls, either — boys often fall for the glamour of ballet get-up, too. Go with it; it's sheer self-expression.

Heads...   shoulders...   knees...

eyes...   ears...   mouth.

and toes...   knees...   and toes...

32 sing together...

Heads, shoulders, knees and toes, knees
and toes/Heads, shoulders, knees and toes,
knees and toes/And eyes and ears and mouth
and nose/Heads, shoulders, knees and toes,
knees and toes. *And then sing it all over again!*

and nose!

33

play
piggy
back

Toddlers need you to direct their
boundless energy and love of physical
fun. So, get down to their level and play
at piggy-back and horse rides. And don't
think this is a game just for dads to
enjoy – mums can get stuck into a
bit of rough and tumble, too!

34

get booked up

Create a book corner, so that your toddler can browse through books whenever she wishes. She's never too young to have stories read to her, but she'll also want to look at books by herself. Books come in all shapes and sizes, with lift-the-flap and pop-up versions being particularly exciting to handle and explore. Your toddler will 'read' them aloud to her dolls or teddies, and to herself.

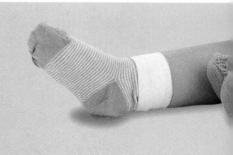

Give

her green fingers

35
water plants

Let her water plants, both indoors and out. Give her her own little watering can to use and be sure to supervise at all times!

37
make a mini garden with her

Give your toddler her own patch of soil to cultivate. Help her plant seeds or make a rockery – she'll love it.

36
give her toy tools

A set of mini garden tools will get her digging and raking. **Take care!** Soil can carry harmful parasites, so keep fingers out of mouths and wash hands thoroughly after gardening.

grow a

cress-head

Take an empty eggshell with the top cut off. Wash it out and leave it to dry. Next, paint on a funny face. Once the paint is dry, put cotton-wool in the bottom of the shell and sprinkle with cress seeds. Soak the cotton-wool with water, put the eggshell on a windowsill, water every day and watch the cress-head grow. You will soon be able to give him a haircut!

Wait and watch...

39

...a giant sunflower grow

Plant several seeds (just in case one or two fail) in a medium-size flower pot. Then place a plastic bag over the pot top and fix with string or an elastic band. Put in a sunny spot and tend every day. As your seedlings grow, move them to a bigger pot.

40 ## ...or a big fat bean

Drop a piece of rolled-up blotting paper into a jam jar, pop a bean between the glass and paper, and drench paper with water. Put jar in a warm, dark place; water as needed.

...or a curly carrot top 41

Cut tops off several carrots and put these in a saucer, cut-side down. Put the saucer in a windowsill and add a little water to it. Keep wet and watch the tops sprout.

Go for a nature walk and...

"let me help

48 ...tidying up

With a toy wheelbarrow, your toddler will enjoy helping you with fetching-and-carrying gardening jobs, such as picking up weeds and grass cuttings.

daddy with..."

49 ...sweeping the path

Toddlers are fascinated by brooms, so buy yours his own mini version. It will be easier and lighter for him to manoeuvre than a big broom, so he'll feel he's doing a really good job.

50 ...clearing leaves

Your little one will enjoy the challenge of loading himself up with an armful of ever-escaping leaves. Make sure he wears gloves.

51 ...washing the car

You'll need your wellies, buckets of soapy water and sponges, and rolled-up sleeves! Never leave your toddler alone with water.

let her dress up

With a few props, a toddler can be anything she wants. Dressing up lets her experiment with 'being' someone else and allows her to 'try out' new feelings as she plays at being busy or important, for example. Collect together clothes, hats, shoes and bags, and watch your toddler show off her innate acting skills.

He can help with the shopping by...

53 ...filling the basket

54 ...holding the shopping list

55 ...pushing the trolley

56 ...weighing the fruit

57

do the spring cleaning...

...and let your little one help. Even the dullest of household chores looks like great fun to your toddler. After all, she will be imitating grown-up behaviour when she offers to 'help' you with sweeping, cleaning or mopping. Give her her own mini dustpan-and-brush set and she will cheerfully potter about, leaving you to get on with your own jobs close by. She'll also enjoy cleaning toy cars with a damp cloth or washing doll's clothes. All the while she will feel she is helping you, too, so encourage her co-operation – it's a powerful antidote to temper tantrums.

58

make her a mini soap star

Never mind the mess it makes — washing dolls and their clothes combines several aspects of creative play. Your toddler will be in her element splashing about in bubbly water, but she's also copying adult behaviour and 'looking after' her toys. And forget any thoughts of domestic drudgery — for your child this is just good, clean fun.

59

hang out the

When it comes to hanging out the washing, it's very useful
to have another pair of hands to help out – particularly when
they're at such a convenient level for the laundry basket!
Toddlers love to get stuck into mounds of freshly washed

washing

clothes and unloading the washing machine makes for great
fun. Always supervise your little helper's enthusiastic efforts
– garments such as pairs of tights and long sleeves represent
a tangle hazard and clothes-pegs can nip little fingers.

give her an ice-cream...

...or whip up your own

Purée 350g (12oz) strawberries. Add 175g (6oz) sugar. Whisk 450ml (¾pt) whipping cream until thick; gently fold this into the purée. Freeze in a plastic container.

62

make juicy ice lollies...

Toddlers love ice lollies – they make the perfect treat on hot
summer days. And they needn't be unhealthy, as you can
incorporate real fruit juice, pieces of fruit and yogurt into
your recipes. All you need to get started is a set of plastic
lolly moulds, some lolly sticks and your chosen ingredients.
For one-flavour lollies, just fill your moulds with pure fruit
juice, squash or yogurt, put in the sticks, and freeze. For
fruit-filled versions, half-fill the moulds with juice or squash
and freeze. Next, add some fruit, fill with the rest of your
base juice, add lolly sticks, and pop in the freezer again.

63

...or a fruit smoothie

To make a smoothie all you need is milk, some fruit – such as strawberries – and natural yogurt. Blend in a food processor. Add honey to taste and a little milk to thin, if needed. For a really creamy drink, add vanilla ice-cream to the initial mix.

64

whizz up a milkshake

For a less rich but still nutritious drink, make a milkshake. It's packed with calcium, protein and, if you use fruit, vitamin C. Just whizz together milk, soft fruit and, if desired, a little honey or sugar to taste. Then pop in a drinking straw and decorate the beaker with a slice of fruit. Chocolate or instant malted drink powder are other taste alternatives to try.

65

go off on
a picnic

Having a picnic is a great way to
spend a sunny afternoon. You
don't have to travel — just
going into the garden with a
blanket or tablecloth is fun.
Invite friends and teddies
and don't forget to…

...pack some tasty

66

mini quiches

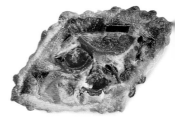

A good cheat is to buy uncooked, unsweetened pastry cases and then to fill them with your own egg-milk quiche mixture topped with cheese and onion, ham or tuna.

67

pitta pockets

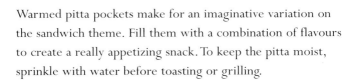

Warmed pitta pockets make for an imaginative variation on the sandwich theme. Fill them with a combination of flavours to create a really appetizing snack. To keep the pitta moist, sprinkle with water before toasting or grilling.

treats to tuck into!

68

sandwiches

Sandwiches can be boring or they can be fun – the choice is yours! For novelty picnic appeal, why not use pastry cutters to cut out sandwiches in an assortment of animal shapes?

69

cup cakes

Set oven to 180°C/350°F/Gas Mark 4. Put 15 paper cases on a baking tray and 100g (4oz) each of self-raising flour, caster sugar and margarine, plus two eggs, in a bowl. Beat until soft. Bake in paper cases for 20–25 minutes. Decorate as desired.

bake a cake together...

Toddlers love to cook – it's something they see you doing so they want to do it, too. But it's also a satisfying, creative process where they see the separate ingredients magically mixed together and turned into something delicious. Rather than bake for real, you can give your toddler a bowl and some flour and water, and let him create his own blobby dough – after all, it's the messy stirring and shaping that really appeals.

and make some biscuits!

Biscuit-baking has the added ingredient of cutting out shapes. Use a simple recipe and let your toddler press out a range of animals with plastic pastry cutters and then decorate the faces with raisin eyes.

72

give her a play pet...

Toddlers often have a natural affinity with baby animals. If yours is addicted to television vet programmes or is pestering you for a puppy of her own, a good initial stage is to encourage her to choose a make-believe pet from one of her selection of cuddly toys. She can 'feed' it, take it for walks and put it to bed — all good disciplines that will enable you to discuss with her what it might be like to have a real pet around the house.

...then get her

Having a pet can give a young child an opportunity to take responsibility (in part!) for another living thing. It provides a focus for young emotions and your toddler will think of her pet as a real friend. Before making your choice of animal, take a trip together to the library so you can read up on different pets and what their care involves.

a real one?

go to the

Whatever your feelings about animals being kept in captivity, zoos do give toddlers the chance to experience close up all the wild creatures that appear in their picture books and on television. Use your trip to talk about colour, shape, size and texture. Compare the size of an elephant with that of a tortoise or a penguin's sleek feathers with a bear cub's furry coat.

zoo!

75

make a paper-plate person

Draw a face on a paper plate, glue on wool hair, then attach plate to a wooden spoon. Make several to create a puppet play.

76

make a silly sock face

Cover your hand with a sock, pushing it between your fingers and thumb to make the mouth, and attach two sticky-dot eyes.

77

make a glove puppet

Cut a finger-size hole in a ping-pong ball; draw on a face. Make a scarf (and a hat if you wish) from felt. Pull on a glove, pop the ball on your finger and tie the scarf at a jaunty angle.

Create cotton

78
a slippery snake

Paint cotton reels, add eyes and a tongue and thread onto string, placing a bead between each reel. Add loops of string to make the snake slither.

79
a jolly caterpillar

Paint reels, sticking paper antennae onto the head reel and adding eyes. Paint blobs on all other reels to make feet. Thread onto string.

reel creatures...

sing together...

Ring-a-ring-o'-roses, [join hands and walk around in a circle]
a pocket full of posies.
A-tishoo, a-tishoo,
we all fall down! [bob down on the floor]

Picking up the daisies, [sit on the floor with hands joined]
picking up the daisies.
A-tishoo, a-tishoo,
we all jump up! [jump up off the floor]

put together a feely bag

Great for parties or for any time, this is a game that is very easily put together and will keep your little one and her friends highly amused. All you need is a pillowcase or cushion cover and a variety of interesting objects to put inside it. Pick items that offer a range of textures for small hands to explore — wooden, metallic, velvety, rubbery, and so on. For shock value and guaranteed giggles, put in the unexpected — try cold cooked spaghetti or a packet of frozen peas!

get out the photos

Looking at photos together is a good quiet-time activity and you'll enjoy talking about the people in the photos as much as your toddler will enjoy hearing about them. Photos make a great talking point and give your child a better understanding of how he fits into the bigger family unit. Show him photos of you when you were a child, as well as pictures of himself when he was a baby.

hand her a paintbrush...

Toddler paintings deserve to command high prices as they're colourful, flamboyant and big! Encourage your child to paint whenever she wants to and, if you like, why not join in yourself? You don't need an easel – just large sheets of paper, a brush and child-safe paints, plus plenty of protective newspaper (painting outside is an even better option if you've a garden and the weather permits). You could always cut down an old shirt to make an artist's smock – this will minimize paint stains on clothes and allow your toddler to give free rein to her creative exuberance.

...and let him put his foot in it

Let him experiment with foot and hand prints. Girls and boys alike love getting messy with paint, but for the sake of your soft furnishings always be around to supervise! The bigger the sheets of paper you can get for your toddler to use the better – this way he can create some large, elaborate patterns. For printing on a small scale, use sponge shapes or potato cut-outs.

build his imagination

As soon as your toddler has the manual dexterity and co-ordination to fit two plastic bricks together, he's off. If there's one type of toy that's designed to have lasting appeal, the humble construction set is it. From towers to traffic lights to trains, he can create whole worlds from one bucket of bricks.

Play ball

86

bowling

Why not devise a game of skittles? Take some empty plastic bottles and half-fill them with water. Arrange them skittle-style and let your toddler bowl them over.

87

throwing

By 18 months, your toddler will probably have sufficient balance to throw a ball. Remove all nearby breakables!

games!

kicking

Some toddlers are natural
footballers, while others
find ball control a little
more challenging. A fun
kick-about usually goes
down well though, but
try to keep it gentle.

Go and get wet...

89

...puddle jumping

Put on waterproof
clothes and wellies and go
out together hunting for
puddles. Toddlers love the
sensation of stamping their
feet and watching the water
splash up. And it's a great
way to let off steam!

90

...raindrop racing

Play the raindrop-racing game – all you need is a wet windowpane! Ask your child to pick a raindrop at the top of the glass and then pick one yourself. See which gets to the bottom first.

91

...umbrella dancing

Take a lead from the movies – put up your umbrellas and find an open space (well away from traffic!). Swing your umbrellas around (avoiding passers-by) and show off your fancy footwork prancing through the puddles.

get in the swing

Swings are fun, whether you're six months or 60 years old. Older toddlers can make the change from a baby swing to a big swing, but you'll need to teach them how to propel themselves and they'll still need a bit of a push.

93

give her bags of fun

A toddler loves a container — whether it's a bag, a box, a basket or a lunch box. She will love hoarding objects inside — packing away her favourite things or clothes for teddy — before carrying them around with her looking very pleased with herself. And it's an activity that will occupy her for ages as she packs and unpacks… packs and unpacks… But beware, if you've lost your keys, check out that bag first — your toddler may have magpie instincts!

94

plump up
the pillows!

There's always time for boisterous play, as
long as you're there to supervise and it's
not just before lights out. Make sure the
hour before bed is spent as quiet time, so
your toddler can wind down after the
excitement of the day.

Let your little sleepyhead...

95
clean her teeth

Make sure your toddler's teeth are brushed twice a day. You'll have to supervise.

97
put on pyjamas

Let her try getting dressed for bed – you may well have to help, but resist if you can.

96
wash her face

Face-washing is never going to be popular, but letting her do it herself may appeal.

98
brush her hair

Let her primp and preen – it doesn't matter if she goes to bed looking like a scarecrow!

...and kiss teddy goodnight...

You can make evenings happier by letting your toddler tuck up teddy as part of her pre-bed wind-down routine. She'll feel very grown-up, and saying night-night to you may be easier for her emotionally if she can relate the idea to her favourite toy.

...ready

for bed

Celebrate the birth of a baby

What is Tommy's Campaign?

Tommy's Campaign is the only UK charity focusing exclusively on healthy pregnancies and babies. Our aim is to give babies the very best start in life by funding pioneering research into premature birth, stillbirth and miscarriage. We also inform parents-to-be about the ways in which they can reduce the risk of having a problem pregnancy.

What is smalltalk ?

Tommy's Campaign has launched a great new club, called 'smalltalk', for parents with babies and toddlers. All you need to do is pay £2 a month (£24 a year) to join. This money will help fund doctors and scientists nationwide in our vital research into the causes of problems in pregnancy.

Join smalltalk and help save a tiny life

If you join smalltalk, you will receive three magazines a year, packed full of hints, tips and advice on parenting – from early-learning ideas for babies through to coping with toddler tantrums, for example. The magazine also features special

readers' offers and competitions and, on first subscribing, you'll receive a free gift.

In addition, we will report back on all the latest news on Tommy's Campaign research – it's the very least we can do. After all, it's only through your generosity and support that we will be able to continue our work towards giving more babies the best possible start in life.

Remember, for just £2 a month you will:

- receive three free issues a year of *smalltalk* magazine
- receive a free Tiny Love toy when you first join
- benefit from special readers' offers and competitions relating to your favourite parenting products
- help fund vital medical research into the causes of problems in pregnancy.

Call free on 0800 096 0508 with your credit card details to SIGN UP NOW!

Tommy's Campaign

Finding the answers to problem pregnancies

Registered charity number 1060508

Acknowledgments

Dorling Kindersley would like to thank the following:

Editorial and design

Dawn Bates and Caroline Greene for their editorial contributions, and Elly King, Bernhard Koppmeyer, Sally Smallwood and Dawn Young for their design assistance.

Photography

Andy Crawford, Mike Dunning, Neil Fletcher, Jo Foord, Mike Good, Steve Gorton, Dave King, Trevor Melton, Ian O'Leary, Daniel Pangbourne, Tim Ridley, Steve Shott and Jerry Young.

Picture credits

Front cover by kind permission of The Stock Market.

Nursery rhymes

The editors have made every effort to establish the identity of possible copyright holders for the nursery rhymes featured, but the investigations strongly suggest that the rhymes used are in the public domain.